LONDON BRIDGE TO EAST CROYDON

Vic Mitchell and Keith Smith

Cover picture details are in caption no. 64.

Design – Deborah Goodridge

First published August 1988

ISBN 0 906520 58 4

© *Middleton Press, 1988*

Typeset by CitySet - Bosham 573270

Published by Middleton Press
        Easebourne Lane
        Midhurst, West Sussex
        GU29 9AZ
        ☎ *(073 081) 3169*

Printed & bound by Biddles Ltd,
        Guildford and Kings Lynn

CONTENTS

MAPS & DIAGRAMS

GEOGRAPHICAL SETTING

The first part of the route is carried on an almost continuous series of brick arches for nearly three miles. When the lines were built the area was occupied by livestock and small market gardens, and was liable to flooding.

Turning south at New Cross Gate, the line climbs the low clay hills which encircle South London from Deptford to Wandsworth and reach a peak of almost 400 ft. above sea level in the vicinity of Crystal Palace.

Croydon is situated on the gravels of the dip slope of the North Downs, at an altitude of 200 ft. and due south of the City of London.

All maps in this album are to the scale of 25″ to 1 mile, unless otherwise stated.

ACKNOWLEDGEMENTS

We are grateful to those mentioned in the captions for the help generously given and also to K. Dungate, C. Hall, R. Randell, E. Staff and N. Stanyon. We thank G. Croughton and N. Langridge for use of tickets from their collections and Mrs. M. Mason and D. Wallis for use of a photograph taken by the late E. Wallis. As ever, our wives have been immensely helpful.

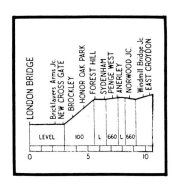

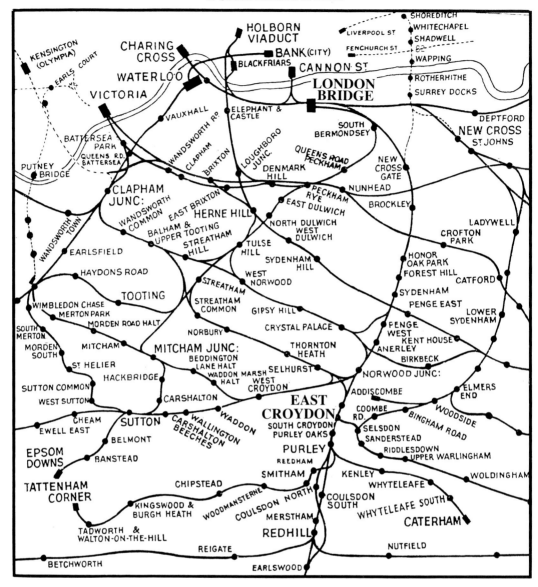

HISTORICAL BACKGROUND

The first London passenger railway south of the Thames was the London & Greenwich, which was opened from Deptford to Spa Road on 8th February 1836 and completed to London Bridge on 14th December of that year.

The London & Croydon Railway came into use on 5th June 1839, trains running between what is now West Croydon and London Bridge, using L&GR tracks north of Corbett's Lane Junction.

The London & Brighton Railway joined the L&CR near the present Norwood Junction and services between Haywards Heath and London Bridge commenced on 12th July 1841. At Croydon, a separate station was provided, which was later named East Croydon. These two companies were amalgamated on 27th July 1846 to form the London, Brighton and South Coast Railway.

The Government believed that only one railway would be required southwards from London and therefore forced the South Eastern Railway to build its line to Dover as a branch from the Brighton line at Reigate Junction (now Redhill). This resulted in acrimony and ludicrous retaliatory acts between the competing companies sharing the route to London Bridge. In 1845, the L&GR became part of the SER, which later built additional termini at Charing Cross and Cannon Street.

On 1st May 1844, the Bricklayers Arms branch came into use, having originally been promoted jointly by the L&CR and the SER as a means of avoiding the L&GR tracks and associated tolls. The terminus was named after a coaching inn in the Old Kent Road, south-east of London Bridge. Regular passenger services ceased in January 1852, but the SER retained the station for freight purposes, the LBSCR (as successor to the L&CR) opening a depot at nearby Willow Walk.

Following the Great Exhibition in Hyde Park in 1851, a group of LBSCR directors decided to re-erect the massive glass hall at Penge Park. The area soon became known as Crystal Palace and a short branch was built to bring materials and workmen from London. The Palace and the branch were opened to the public on 10th June 1854. The line was extended to Wandsworth Common on 30th November 1856 and later to Battersea and Victoria. In 1857, a spur was added to permit direct running from the south to this line and, on 1st December 1862, the shorter route to Victoria via Selhurst and Norbury came into use.

The railway map was completed during the 1860s when the South London line from Victoria joined the route near South Bermondsey in 1866, and the East London Railway reached the New Cross stations of the SER and LBSCR in 1869.

* * * * *

A line that never appeared on the passenger network was the freight-only branch opened by the LBSCR from New Cross to Deptford Wharf on 2nd July 1849. It remained in use until 1st January 1964.

II. Evolution of the railways to London Bridge. (Railway Magazine)

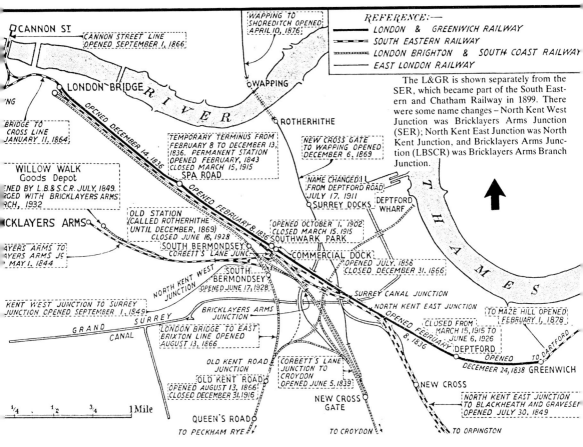

PASSENGER SERVICES

The first L&BR timetable showed eight trains on weekdays between London Bridge and Croydon (East), and additional services were provided by the L&CR north of Norwood Junction, then Jolly Sailor.

In 1842, the L&BR frequency was reduced to six on weekdays, with three on Sundays. A steady increase took place from 1843, which would be tedious to recount in detail. We therefore quote a few notable features.

The completion of the East London Line to Shoreditch in 1876, enabled through services between Liverpool Street and East Croydon to operate for over 30 years.

During the period of antagonism between the SER and the LBSCR, the SER several times altered the timings of its up business trains so that they preceded the LBSCR trains by a few minutes and scooped up passengers from the suburban stations. The LBSCR developed an interesting "skip-stop" service which lasted until electrification. It is shown below.

Electrification of the route brought regular interval timetables, at least outside the peak hours, and the line has since had one of the most comprehensive train services in any part of London, particularly in terms of frequency and variety of destinations. This was improved still further on 16th May 1988, with the commencement of Thameslink services to the Bedford line, with two trains per hour from East Croydon via London Bridge and two via Herne Hill.

Train From a.m.	Norwood Junction	Anerley	Penge	Sydenham	Forest Hill	Honor Oak Park	Brockley	New Cross	London Bridge
7.36 Cheam	7.58	8.02	....	8.05	....	8.09	8.12	8.15	8.22
7.32 Victoria	....	8.09	8.11	....	8.16	....	....	....	8.26
8.10 W Croydon	8.15	....	....	....	....	....	....	....	8.31
8.20 Crystal Palace	....	....	....	8.24	....	8.28	8.31	8.34	8.41
8.23 Crystal Palace	....	....	....	8.27	8.30	8.33	8.36	8.39	8.45
8.11 Cheam	....	....	....	....	....	....	....	....	8.49
8.38 Crystal Palace	....	....	....	8.42	....	8.47	8.50	....	8.58
8.42 Crystal Palace	....	....	....	....	8.48	8.51	....	....	9.01
8.23 Coulsdon	8.45	8.49	8.51	....	....	....	8.58	9.01	9.07
8.49 W Croydon	....	....	....	....	9.00	9.03	....	9.08	9.15
8.58 Crystal Palace	....	....	....	9.02	9.05	....	9.10	9.13	9.20
8.18 London Bridge	8.59	9.03	9.05	....	9.10	9.13	....	9.18	9.24
8.53 Streatham Com.	....	9.10	9.12	9.15	....	....	9.21	....	9.29
9.08 Wallington	....	....	....	....	....	....	....	....	9.32
9.21 Crystal Palace	....	....	....	9.25	9.28	9.31	9.34	9.37	9.44
9.20 W Croydon	....	9.27	9.29	9.32	9.35	9.38	....	....	9.47
9.15 Sutton	9.34	....	....	....	....	....	....	....	9.51

Trains also leave Norwood Jct for London Bridge on the Main Line at 8.20am (8.0am Coulsdon) and 9.21am (8.59 Coulsdon).

Electric Traction

Electrification of the South London line brought overhead conductor wires into London Bridge station prior to the commencement of electric services to Victoria on 1st December 1909. The system was extended as follows:-

Battersea Park - Balham - Crystal Palace   12th May 1911
Crystal Palace - Norwood Jn. - Selhurst   1st June 1912
Balham - Selhurst - Coulsdon North   1st April 1925

Thus the route was covered by three short lengths of overhead equipment. Conductor rails came into use between London Bridge and Crystal Palace (Low Level) on 25th March 1928 and were extended through Norwood Junction and East Croydon to Coulsdon North on 17th June 1928.

ATMOSPHERIC TRAINS

Following the success of the Dublin and Kingstown Railway's atmospheric system (which ran for 12 years), the L&CR decided to lay a third track between Croydon (now West) and Forest Hill, and to include a 15″ diameter vacuum tube between the rails. Ornate pumping houses were built at Croydon, Norwood and Forest Hill, all linked by electric telegraph. These pumped air from the tube and caused a piston, attached to the leading vehicle, to be sucked along at speeds supposedly of 70mph, although 44½mph was the average for the inspector's journey prior to the opening on 19th January 1846.

Operation was extended north to New Cross in February 1847 but the tube never reached London Bridge or Epsom as planned because the newly formed LBSCR decided to abandon the system in May 1847, on the grounds of inflexibility and high cost of operation, maintenance and extension.

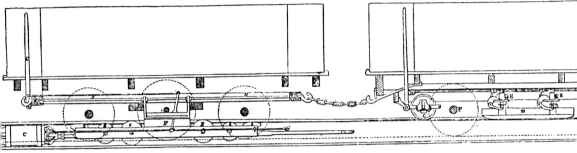

III Atmospheric haulage. The left hand vehicle is attached to the piston C by means of a plate F which passes through a valved slot in the top of the vacuum tube. The plate and piston are secured to an assembly carried on four wheels in the tube. The two larger wheels E lift the leather longitudinal valve on the top of the tube as the train progresses. The right-hand vehicle followed and has a wheel C to shut the valve and a heater D, theoretically to reseal the valve in its wax jointing. This must have been of limited effect at speed!

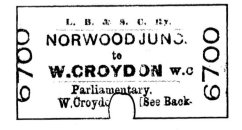

IV. Atmospheric tube. The piston A, which was capped with leather in lieu of piston rings, is shown inside the tube, with the leather valve B open and the bent connecting plate passing through the slot. C is a lever which could be used when an emergency stop was required. It opened the valve D in the piston, allowing air to pass through it. Normally, the train brakes were used.

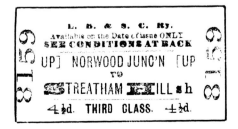

LONDON BRIDGE

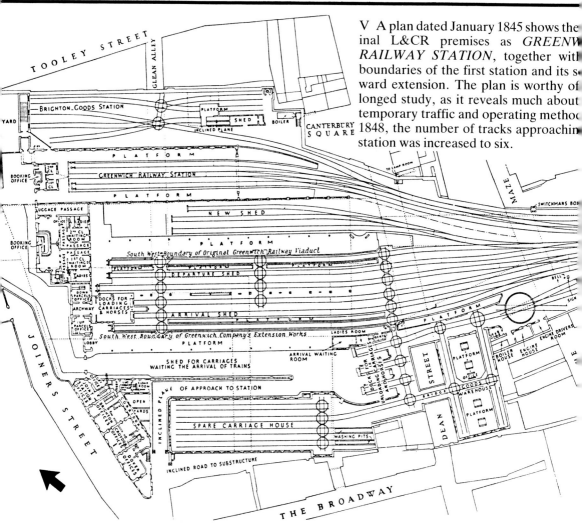

V A plan dated January 1845 shows the [orig]inal L&CR premises as *GREENW[ICH] RAILWAY STATION*, together wit[h the] boundaries of the first station and its s[outh]ward extension. The plan is worthy of pro[longed] study, as it reveals much about [con]temporary traffic and operating method[s. By] 1848, the number of tracks approachin[g the] station was increased to six.

1. The L&GR terminus was situated in the vicinity of the present platforms 7-8 and it soon became congested with L&CR trains, as a 15-minute interval service was operated to Greenwich from the outset. A separate station for Croydon passengers was opened to the north of the original. With the addition of separate tracks for the L&CR, the two companies swopped stations in 1840, to eliminate the crossing of trains. The station illustrated was opened on 3rd February 1844 but was replaced about five years later when further expansion took place. (British Rail)

2. Considerable alterations took place in the years prior to the opening of the SER's line to Charing Cross on 11th January 1864. The LBSCR's side of the station evolved into this fine symmetrical structure, photographed in 1882 when Terrier tanks were in their infancy. (Bluebell Archives)

3. The final widening of the approach lines was in 1901, when the number of tracks was increased to eleven. Looking over the double-sided coal stage and the turntable, we see North Box. In this and the next picture there are some fish-tailed signal arms which preceded the ringed variety for allowing a second train into an occupied platform. They were lowered when the line was clear to the buffers. (J.R.W. Kirkby collection)

4. The complexities of LBSCR headcodes are evident in this view from about 1904, in which everyone is looking at the camera except the lampman on the carriage roof. The short ringed arms were for outward shunt movements. (E. Jackson collection)

5. A rare interior view reveals the fine tracery of the stanchion brackets and the complexity of the truss design, together with Royal Mail road transport of the Edwardian era. (NRM)

6. Buses for Bank and Maida Vale stand outside the Turkish Baths and behind them is the 150-room LBSCR Terminus Hotel, which was built in 1861. It included a library, a billiard room, a smoking room, a ladies' coffee room and lifts – an innovation at that time. (R. Resch collection)

7. From left to right – South Box, North Box and the SECR Box. The overhead catenary carried 6700 volts AC and was first used on 1st December 1909 for the Victoria service via the South London Line. (Lens of Sutton)

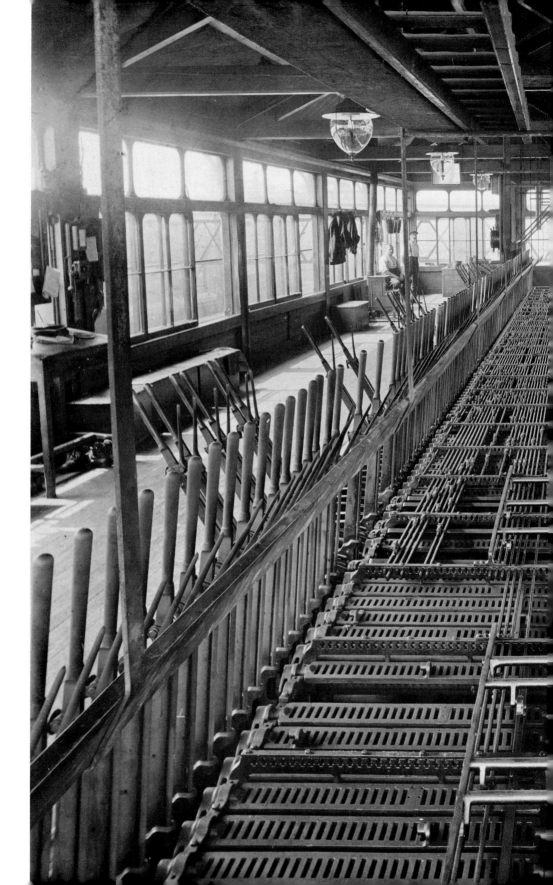

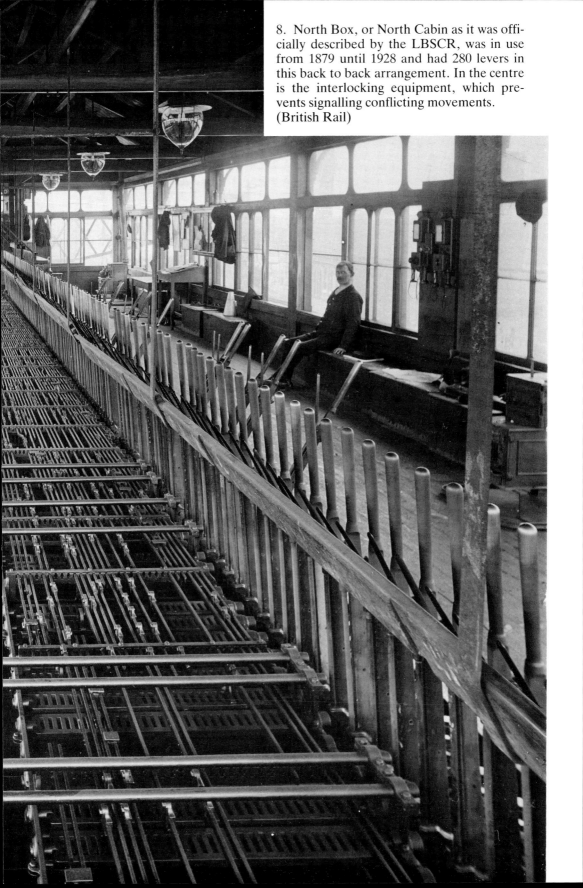

8. North Box, or North Cabin as it was officially described by the LBSCR, was in use from 1879 until 1928 and had 280 levers in this back to back arrangement. In the centre is the interlocking equipment, which prevents signalling conflicting movements. (British Rail)

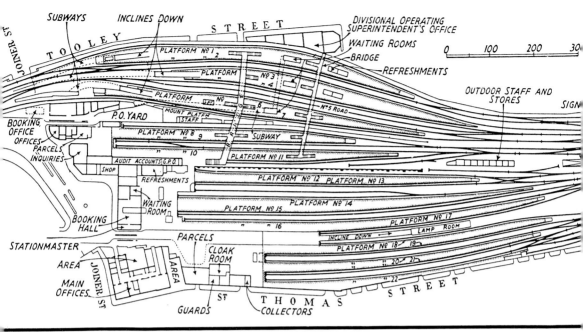

VI The 1937 plan reveals that there was no platform numbered 5 but there were 22 platforms altogether – Mount Platform had no number as it was only used for mailbags. (Railway Magazine)

9. The crew gaze at an obstinate injector prior to departure with the 10.10 am to Portsmouth Harbour on 1st July 1938, two days before this service was electrified. Main line electrification to Brighton and West Worthing had taken place 5½ years earlier. (J.G. Sturt)

10. The scene changed dramatically on 29th December 1940 when the former Terminus Hotel was destroyed by German bombs. We are looking northwards across St. Thomas's Street, the station approach canopies, seen in picture no.6, being on the left of this one. (British Rail)

11. The signalman's view on 14th May 1959 includes class E4 0-6-2T no. 32474 leaving platform 16 and three centuries of Guy's Hospital – 18c. chapel visible above the last van; 19c spire of the medical block and a 20c. extension, both on the left. (R.C. Riley)

12. Colour light signalling was introduced on 17th June 1928 when this signal box was commissioned. In some cases, the new signals were attached to the old AC electrification gantries. This photograph was taken from the end of platform 14 in August 1971. (E. Wilmshurst)

13. Another 1971 picture shows the shortest platforms (17 and 18) and the long-forgotten ramp to street level between them. Subsequently, the platforms were lengthened by eliminating the roadway; 17 became 14 and the ramp was filled in. The redundant locomotive water tank is also visible. (E. Wilmshurst)

14. The wall on the left separated the LBSCR and SECR stations until 1928, when a hole was made in it and a ticket barrier installed near the buffer stops of platform 12 (now 9). This 1974 view shows the then new footbridge built to link all the platforms. (British Rail)

15. Since railways began, the speedy transport of newspapers has been a regular source of revenue but BR ended this traffic in July 1988. Electro-diesel no. 73126 stands at platform 13 with newspaper vans for Brighton on 27th June 1982. (J.S. Petley)

16. The 1928 signal box was superseded by a panel box on 20th July 1975, which replaced 16 signal boxes. It was built on the site of the lines that once led to platforms 20 to 22 and now controls 47 route miles. This May 1987 photograph shows offices standing where three platforms were once located. (A.C. Mott)

BRICKLAYERS ARMS

17. Three reasons are given for the opening of this station. Firstly, avoidance of L&GR tolls. Secondly, more convenient road access to the West End for passengers. Thirdly, insufficient freight handling facilities at London Bridge. Only the latter reason stood the test of time and services were withdrawn from the passenger timetable after only eight years. (Lens of Sutton)

18. Flags were flying on 9th June 1953 for the Coronation and posters displayed for excursions from London Bridge. The tracks in the foreground had ceased to carry trams in the previous year. (British Rail)

19. Looking north-west from Upper Grange Road bridge, we see what the SR later described as area 'F' of the yard, it being divided into 13 sections. On the left are cattle pens and a brace of overtype steam wagons, while on the right we see the main goods inward shed. (NRM)

20. Looking slightly to the right of the previous picture (at an earlier date and through an inferior lens), we see two of the three SECR locomotive sheds and two coaling cranes. Before electrification, up to 150 engines were based here, there still being about 100 when the depot was modernised prior to WWII. There were only 16 left when closure took place in 1962. (S.C. Nash collection)

VII The 1875 survey gives an impression of the extent of the depot, with its almost countless wagon turntables. The large number of stables reflects the number of horses required, not only for cartage but also for shunting. The three rows of houses northeast of the approach lines were demolished in 1892 to make way for a 23-road shed, which increased the capacity of the LBSCR's Willow Walk Depot. Lower left are double tram tracks in the Old Kent Road.

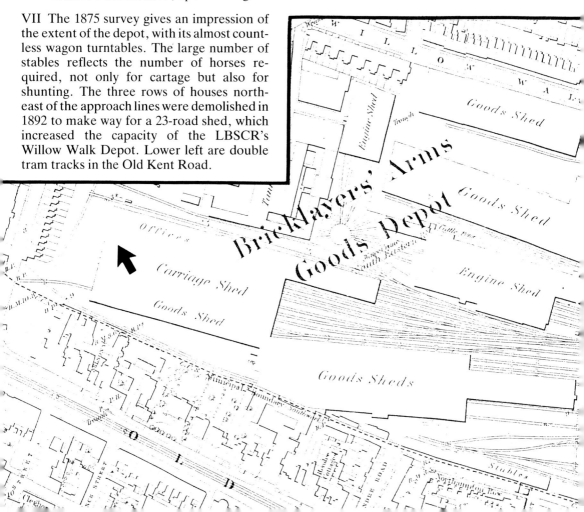

21. A view west from St. James Road bridge shows Willow Walk Junction Box on the right and the main sheds of the depot, ½ mile distant. Willow Walk was amalgamated operationally with Bricklayers Arms on 7th March 1932. (NRM)

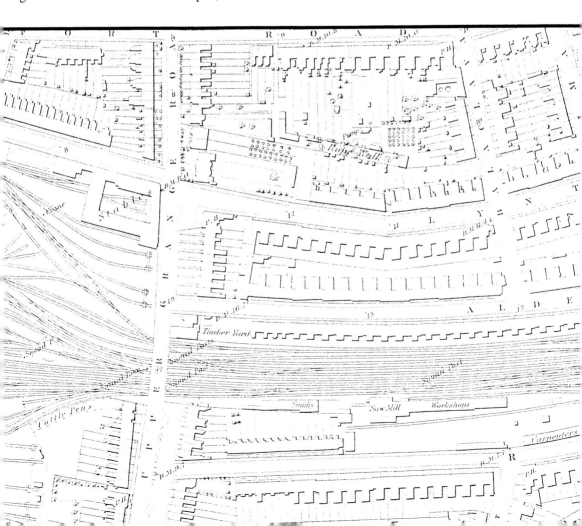

22. The 1892 extension to Willow Walk depot was adjacent to Lynton Road and was devastated by enemy bombing on 17th September 1940. The SR designated this 'L' shed and used it for goods outwards. They also ran excursions from Bricklayers Arms on summer Sundays in 1932-39. (British Rail)

VIII. The 1932 diagram shows the usage of the sheds and the extensive stables. The tracks of the eastern engine shed were later extended to the turntable, which was increased to 65ft. diameter. Goods traffic ceased on 1st August 1977 but coal and parcel traffic continued for a time.

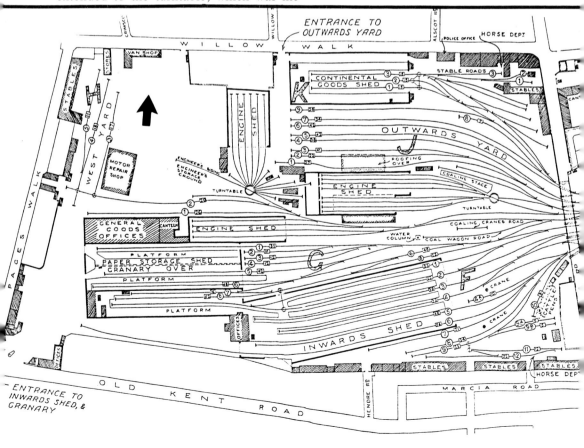

23. The passenger entrance was at the south-west corner of the buildings and was in use as offices when photographed in March 1957.
(P. Hay)

IX. 'L' shed was unusual in having the sidings enter through the side wall instead of the end, a feature not obvious in the photo-graph. The figures in rectangles indicate the number of wagons that could be accommo-dated.

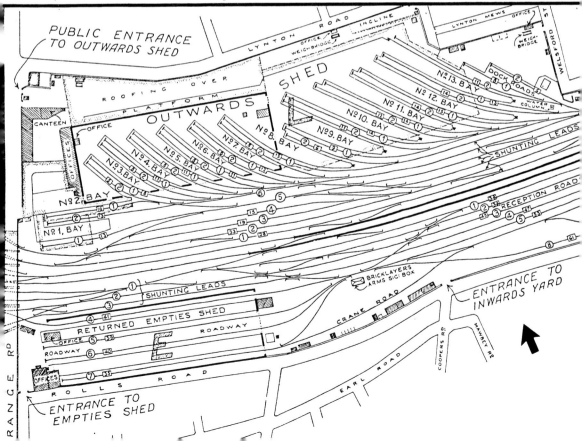

24. Nine tracks passed under St. James Road bridge, from which this photograph was taken in November 1954. In the background is Paterson Park and Lynton Road. (R.C. Riley)

X. The London Bridge lines are on the left and the Bricklayers Arms branch is at the bottom of the map. Southwark Park station is on the SECR main line. This 1916 map continues on the page after next and is to the scale of 15″ to 1 mile.

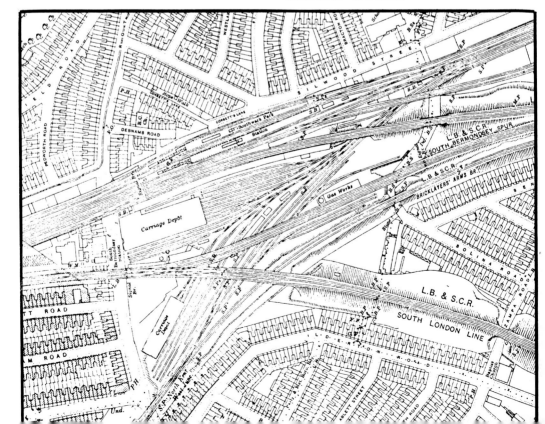

25. The terminus of the one mile long branch is behind us, as we stand on the bridge over Rotherhithe New Road and look at North Kent West Junction Box, formerly Bricklayers Arms Junction. Diverging to the left are the lines to New Cross and those on the right lead to New Cross Gate, both first passing under the South London Line. (J. Scrace)

26. Class C2X 0–6–0 no. 32552 hauls vans under the arches carrying the Bermondsey Spur which links the South London Line with the main line to New Cross Gate. This is also carried on arches but just out of view, on the right. Rotherhithe Road carriage depot is seen in April 1957. The shed had eight roads and the locomotive is obscuring the view of the four adjacent sidings. (P. Hay)

27. A photograph from the main line to New Cross Gate in 1959 shows the Bricklayers Arms – New Cross tracks adjacent to the gas tank wagons. The gas was used in steam-hauled restaurant cars and was produced in the building on the left. The arches carry the Bermondsey Spur and, in the background, a down train can be seen in South Bermondsey station. (P. Hay)

XI. Continued from the page before last, the lifting bridge carrying the Deptford Wharf branch over the Surrey Canal is marked near the top of the left hand page. Reference to the evolution map in the introduction will help to identify the other lines.

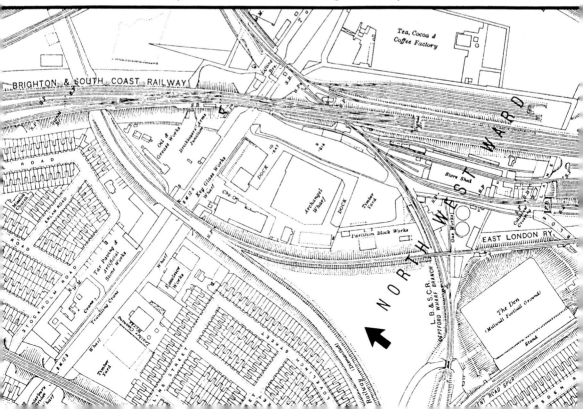

28. The former LBSCR Cold Blow Signal Works is featured here. It took its name from Cold Blow Lane, seen in the foreground, as did the signal box on the right. This north- ward view shows the gates over the Deptford Wharf branch, which became single track before passing under the main line. (E. Jackson collection)

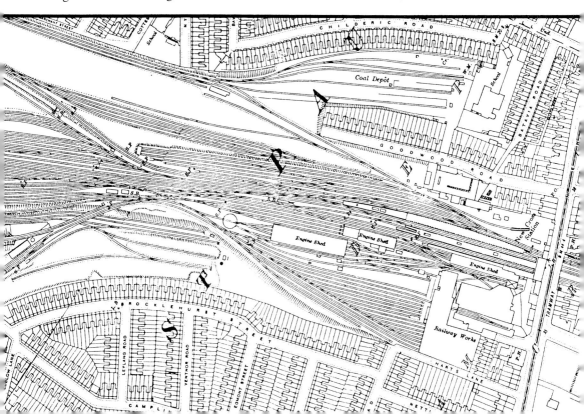

29. Looking south in 1958 from the foot-bridge seen on the right of the previous picture, we see the single line connection from New Cross Gate station and three lines passing under the Old Kent Road Spur. (D. Cullum)

→

30. Looking north on 27th June 1944, the effects of enemy action are being rectified, only feet from the bridge over the Surrey Canal. Beyond Bricklayers Arms Box, the Bermondsey Spur diverges to the left. The arches on the right carry some of the former SECR tracks to New Cross. (British Rail)

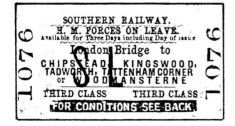

SOUTHERN RAILWAY.
H. M. FORCES ON LEAVE.
Available for Three Days including Day of issue
London Bridge to
CHIPSTEAD KINGSWOOD,
TADWORTH, TATTENHAM CORNER
or WOODMANSTERNE
THIRD CLASS   THIRD CLASS
FOR CONDITIONS SEE BACK

→

31. The box seen in the previous picture was replaced by this one on 8th October 1950. It remained in use until 20th July 1975 and was photographed on 4th September 1975 as the 10.12 Hither Green to Norwood Yard freight passes by, behind no. 73115. (J. Scrace)

DEPTFORD WHARF

32. Initially, the LBSCR only had access to water frontage at Kingston, near Shoreham in Sussex. Opening of a branch, less than a mile long, on 2nd July 1849 gave access to the busy River Thames. When photographed in 1958, the fan of sidings was at its optimum, with coal as the main traffic. (D. Cullum)

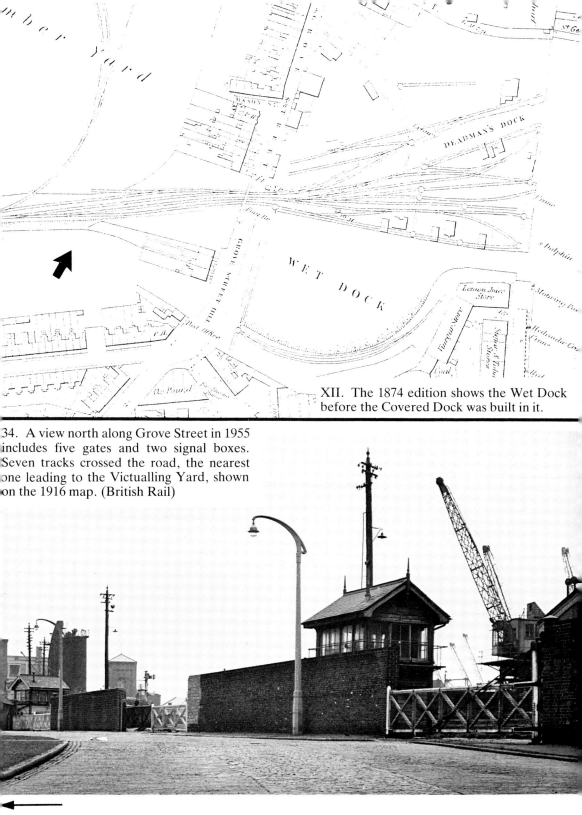

XII. The 1874 edition shows the Wet Dock before the Covered Dock was built in it.

34. A view north along Grove Street in 1955 includes five gates and two signal boxes. Seven tracks crossed the road, the nearest one leading to the Victualling Yard, shown on the 1916 map. (British Rail)

33. A covered dock with overhead travelling cranes was a feature of later developments. This 1955 picture includes a mineral wagon on the left and imported timber on the right, which had come from North America and Scandinavia. (British Rail)

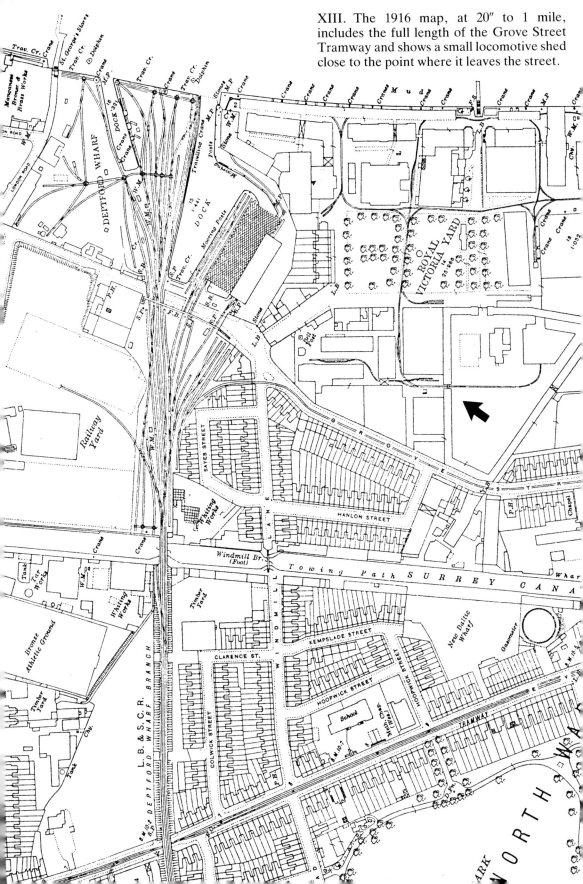

XIII. The 1916 map, at 20″ to 1 mile, includes the full length of the Grove Street Tramway and shows a small locomotive shed close to the point where it leaves the street.

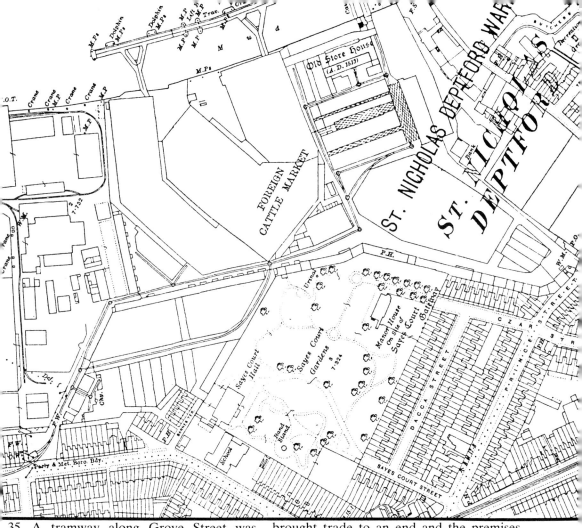

35. A tramway along Grove Street was opened on 15th December 1900 to give rail access to the City of London Corporation's Foreign Cattle Market and it was operated by their own Maudslay petrol locomotive. WWI brought trade to an end and the premises became an army depot. The junction was then relaid to allow LBSCR locomotives direct access to the line. (Lens of Sutton)

36. With our back to New Cross Gate we see the Grove Street crossing gates in the distance and Crow Catchpole's sidings on the left. These were used for the conveyance of creosote. Grove Street tramway to the Supply Reserve Depot curves away sharply on the right. Note the long footbridge, necessary due to the prolonged obstruction of the highway by shunting movements. (D. Cullum)

37. The branch was carried over the Surrey Canal by an unusual lifting bridge, designed by the locomotive department. This northward view in 1958 shows the former SECR main line in the background. All but the framework of the signal box was severely damaged by enemy action on 26th June 1944. (D. Cullum)

38. The Union Lighterage Co's. tank lighters *Clare* and *Arran* pass under the raised span on 2nd May 1961. The former LBSCR main line is in the background. *Surrey Waterways* (Middleton Press) contains information on the Surrey Canal, formerly the Grand Surrey Canal. The branch closed on 1st January 1964. (P. Hay)

NEW CROSS GATE

39. The suffix "Gate" was added by the SR on 9th July 1923, to end confusion with the former SECR station. Opened by the L&CR, the station has always been of importance, being located on the main London - Kent highway. A down express speeds through behind class B1 0-4-2 *Hampden*, one of the "Gladstones". (R.C. Riley collection)

41. The East London Railway was leased jointly by the LBSCR, SER, LCDR, District and Metropolitan Railways and was purchased by the SR in 1925. It was electrified on 31st March 1913 for use by Metropolitan trains, after which there were no through trains between Croydon and Liverpool Street. This scene from October 1951 includes a coal train from Deptford Wharf and an ex-District Railway EMU of 1906 vintage, still running with hand-operated sliding doors. (P. Hay)

◄━━━━━

40. A photograph from the austere days of 1948 typifies the neglected state in which the railways were when taken over by the government in that year. The roads were no better – setts are missing in the tram tracks. (British Rail)

L. B. & S. C. Ry.
Available on the DATE of issue ONLY
This Ticket is issued subject to the Regulations
& Conditions stated in the Company's Time
Tables & Bills.

NEW CROSS
TO
FOREST HILL f.h.

3d. 3rd Class. 3d.

704   48014

L. B. & S. C. Ry.
Available on the DATE of issue ONLY
This Ticket is issued subject to the Regulations
& Conditions stated in the Company's Time
Tables & Bills.

NEW CROSS
TO
BALHAM ba
VIA CRYSTAL PALACE STATION
7d. THIRD CLASS. 7d.

2705   2705

SOUTHERN RAILWAY.
Available for CHILD under 12 Years of age
Available on the DATE of issue ONLY.
This ticket is issued subject to the Regulations
& Conditions stated in the Company's Time
Tables & Bills.

NEW CROSS GATE
TO
NORWOOD JUN. & SOUTH NORWOOD
THIRD CLASS.
4½d.   Fare.   4½d.

0610   0610

SOUTHERN RAILWAY.
Issued subject to the Bye-laws, Regulations &
Conditions in the Company's Bills and Notices.

New Cross Gate to
New Cross Gate   New Cross Gate
East Croydon   East Croydon
EAST CROYDON

THIRD CLASS   THIRD CLASS
Fare 1/2   Fare 1/2
NOT TRANSFERABLE.

4785   4785

← 42. Looking north from the station's covered footbridge in 1958, we find electric stock berthed on the site of one of the former steam sheds. The nearest set is one of the wooden-bodied type originally provided in 3-car configuration for the first conductor rail services. (D. Cullum)

43. A 1958 southward panorama includes the East London Up Junction Box (used for East London and Deptford Wharf connections only) and the 1950 New Cross Gate Box. Behind it are sidings once owned by the GER and used as a coal depot. In front of it is the double track used by LT trains to Whitechapel. (D. Cullum)

44. Another southward view in 1958 shows clearly the commencement of the 2½ mile climb at 1 in 100 up to Forest Hill. At most stations, the up platform is no.1, but here they are 4 and 5. Another unusual feature is that the roof profiles are different on every platform. (D. Cullum)

45. A 1987 photograph portrays the third style of platform canopy and a Metropolitan Line train, bearing an incorrect destination. There is now no connection between LT and BR tracks. The four electrified and four non-electrified carriage sidings, obscured by the Whitechapel train, join the down local line south of the LT buffer stops. (A.C. Mott)

NEW CROSS
LOCOMOTIVE SHED

46. The L&CR established their shed and workshops at this then rural location, creating an early roundhouse (which was actually octagonal). Three rectangular locomotive sheds were added and while the works moved to Brighton, additional carriage sheds were built here. The Octagon was burnt out in 1844 and this is the scene on 30th October 1863 when the shed nearest to the station was blown down. (NRM)

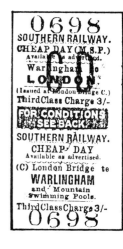

47. A poor but interesting photograph shows Middle Shed in the centre and New Shed on the right. The lines on the extreme right lead to the carriage works. There were once 21 sidings to the right of New Shed – see the map below picture 28. (Lens of Sutton)

48. Middle Shed and New Shed had three and four roads respectively. On the left, class D3 no. 396 is yet unrebuilt, thus dating the photograph as prior to 1906. (J.R.W. Kirkby collection)

49. Class E2 no. B107 and E1 no. B142 stand outside New Shed in about 1930, at a time when the depot had around 90 locomotives, 60 of which were freight or tank engines. The allocation was reduced during the 1930s, by transfer to Bricklayers Arms and Norwood Junction. (R.C. Riley collection)

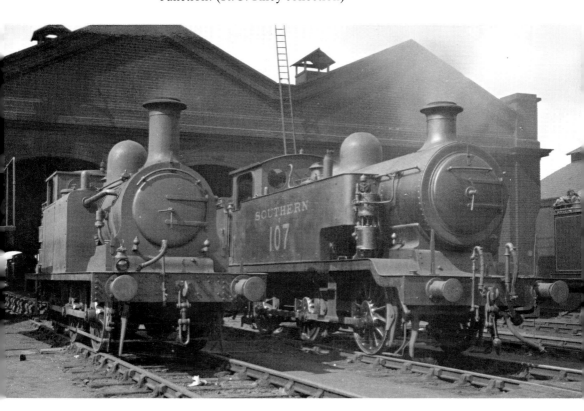

50. The sheds damaged by natural forces were repaired but by 1938 the roundhouse had lost most of its slates again. It was known as The Rooter and had for several decades only housed Terriers used on the East and South London services. On the left and adjacent to platform 5 is the Croydon Shed. (R.C. Riley)

51. The relationship of Middle Shed to the two up platforms is clear in this October 1949 photograph. The depot officially closed on 14th June 1947 but continued to stable locomotives until 1951. (D. Clayton)

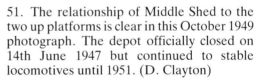

52. South of New Cross Gate the quadruple main line enters a long cutting as it ascends to Forest Hill. One of the two sidings in the foreground was retained and electrified for empty carriage movement. Class E4 no. 32474 was on its last main line freight duty on 2nd May 1963, hauling the 1.44 pm New Cross Gate to Norwood. New Cross Gate yard closed on 9th November 1967. (S.C. Nash)

BROCKLEY

53. Opened on 6th March 1871 in response to expanding residential development, the LBSCR did not monopolise the district for long. In the following year, the LCDR opened their Brockley Lane station but it was closed on 1st January 1917. The station building is seen on the top right of this view of the 12 noon London Bridge to Brighton hurrying past a slow train in 1905.
(R.C. Riley collection)

```
  2 9 1 6          L. & S. C. RY.
              Available on the Date of issue ONLY.
              SEE CONDITIONS AT BACK.
              D'N] BROCKLEY [D'N          5 6 1 9 2
              No. 6]           TO
  2 9 1 6     New Cross. n.c.
              1d.   THIRD CLASS.   1d
```

55. Class D1 0–4–2T no. B218 arrives with a mixture of 6-wheelers and bogies on 2nd August 1926. The bridges are – public footway, passenger, Lewisham - Nunhead line and Endwell Road, in the background.
(H.C. Casserley)

```
              L. B. & S. C. RY.
              Available on the Date of issue ONLY.
              SEE CONDITIONS AT BACK.
              D'N] BROCKLEY [D'N
              No. 6]          TO
              London Bridge.lb.
              3d.   THIRD CLASS.   3d
```

54. The fireman stoops for some coal as his class D1 waits to leave with a down local. The signalman looks out at his signals which are in slotted posts with independent rotating lamps. (J.R.W. Kirkby collection)

56. A northward view in 1949 emphasises the size of the platform canopies. A rectangular CLASP building now stands on the down side, unusual in being two-storied, with the booking office at road level. (D. Clayton)

58. Schools class no. 30915 *Brighton* was in charge of the 5.25 pm from London Bridge on 29th August 1961 as it lifted its ten coaches up the 1 in 100 on their way to Tonbridge or Reading – an operational legacy from the SECR. The clay sides of the cutting have slipped many times – the bulge below the telegraph poles is evidence of past movement. (J. Scrace)

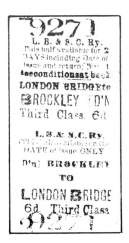

← ——— 57. The 5.25 pm London Bridge to Reading South on 22nd May 1952 was hauled by U class no. 31618, coupled to a tender still marked *SOUTHERN*. This train shed a portion for Tonbridge at Redhill and arrived at its remote destination at 7.59 pm. (C.R.L. Coles)

59. As at Norbury, part of the cost of the station was paid for by local estate developers. In this case £1000 was paid towards the station which opened on 1st April 1886. Class D1 no. 623 is seen on the up main line in about 1914. The coaches are the London Bridge portion of a Victoria train from Hastings that was divided at East Croydon. (Lens of Sutton)

60. GER 2–4–2T no. 101 runs into the down platform with GER stock on a Liverpool Street to Croydon service. The LBSCR ceased participating in this operation in 1885. (E.R. Lacey collection)

61. Details of the down platform accommodation can be observed as class D3 no. 385 heads a "Roundabout" London Bridge to London Bridge via Streatham, Selhurst and Norwood Junction.
(J.R.W. Kirkby collection)

62. A down freight enters the station behind this class E3 no. 459, towards the end of the LBSCR era. The bridge in the background was demolished at about this time.
(E.R. Lacey collection)

63. Long lost features are the upper quadrant signals, the gas lights and the signal box, which closed on 8th October 1950. The signal bracket makes an unusual location to pose for a photograph. (E. Jackson collection)

64. Class I3 no. 32075 pounds up the bank with the 5.20 pm London Bridge to Tunbridge Wells West on 15th June 1950. A local electric is seen under the new concrete signal bracket. (S.C. Nash)

FOREST HILL

65. Opened by the L&CR as "Dartmouth Arms", the name was changed in 1845. Hamilton-Ellis described the tower as "LBSC-Romanesque and decidedly sumptuous". The bus driver projects his hand as a tram grinds up the hill, in this undated postcard view. (Lens of Sutton)

XIV. The 1916 survey reveals the great extent of the station buildings, on both sides, and the remoteness of the goods yard from them. The yard closed on 4th May 1964.

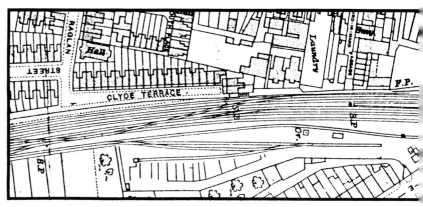

66. The buildings seen in the previous photograph are completely obscured by this one, which was to the south of them. We are viewing the up local platform from the up main. (NRM)

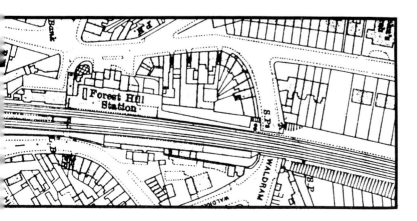

67. Class D3 no. 394 leaves Forest Hill on the down local line with a train for Crystal Palace. In the distance is Forest Hill Box, opposite which there was a ladder crossover for returning the bank engines of down freight trains. (J.R.W. Kirkby collection)

→

69. The up "City Limited" speeds through, hauled by class H1 no. B40 *St. Catherine's Point*. A milk van is behind the tender and milk churns abound on the up local platform. (D. Cullum collection)

L. B. & S. C. RY.
Available on the DATE of issue ONLY
This Ticket is issued subject to the Regulations
& Conditions stated in the Company's Time
Tables & Bills

8420 **FOREST HILL** 8420
Series 33   TO   [Series 33
Sydenham. sy
1d. THIRD CLASS. 1d.

SOUTHERN RAILWAY.
This ticket is issued subject to the Company's
Bye-laws, Regulations and Conditions in their
Time Tables, Notices and Book of Regulations.
Available on DAY of issue ONLY.

4072 **FOREST HILL** to 4072
Forest Hill   Forest Hill
Anerley   Anerley
ANERLEY
THIRD CLASS   THIRD CLASS
Fare 3d.   Fare 3d.

L. B. & S. C. RY.
Available on the DATE of issue ONLY.
This Ticket is issued subject to the Regulations
& conditions stated in the Company's Time
Tables & Bills

8941 **FOREST HILL** 8941
Series 19   TO   Series 19
LONDON BRIDGE l.b.
5½d. THIRD CLASS. 5½d.

68. Ex-SECR class F1 no. A187 roars through with a down express on 18th December 1926, the photograph giving us the opportunity to see the access to the island platform from the subway. (H.C. Casserley)

70. The scene on 23rd June 1944, when clearing up was about to commence. Part of the 1883 building on the right was patched up and remained in use for many years after the war. A section of canopy lies neatly on the platform, as if laid out by an undertaker. (British Rail)

SOUTHERN RAILWAY.
This ticket is issued subject to the Company's Bye-laws, Regulations and Conditions in their Time Tables, Notices and Book of Regulations. Available on DAY of issue ONLY.

Forest Hill   to

Forest Hill   Forest Hill
Honor Oak Park   Honor Oak Park

HONOR OAK PARK

THIRD CLASS   THIRD CLASS
Fare 1½d.   Fare 1½d.

4627   4627

71. Purists raised their eyes when the SR erected these up starting signals. The LBSCR set the up main arm higher than the local and only the latter was repeated at the lower level. These were photographed in November 1949. (Pamlin Prints)

72. The down side buildings were slightly less pompous. The awning boasts *SOUTHERN RAILWAY* but the poster boards admit that British Railways are in control. A booking office was available therein for stations south only – the near end of the building was let as a timber merchant's office. (Lens of Sutton)

L. B. S. C. RY.
Available... ...ate of issue ONLY.
This ticket issued subject to the Regulations
& Conditions stated in the Company's Time
Tables & Bills.
FOREST HILL
TO
BROCKLEY bk
THIRD CLASS.
3½d.   Revised Fare.   3½d.
0675   0675

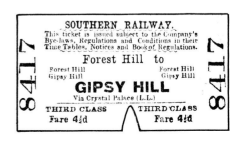

SOUTHERN RAILWAY.
This ticket is issued subject to the Company's
Bye-laws, Regulations and Conditions in their
Time Tables, Notices and Book of Regulations.
Forest Hill   to
Forest Hill   Forest Hill
Gipsy Hill   Gipsy Hill
GIPSY HILL
Via Crystal Palace (L.L.)
THIRD CLASS   THIRD CLASS
Fare 4½d   Fare 4½d
8417   8417

73. This curiously cantilevered box had parts exposed that were kept private in most boxes. It was by milepost 5¾, just south of the station and was replaced on 8th October 1950, having been photographed a week earlier. (D. Cullum)

→

75. The 5.25 pm London Bridge to Reading South was a popular train to photograph but seldom was it double headed. U class no. 31796 and Schools class no. 30916 *Whitgift* pass the 1950 signal box and goods yard headshunt on 9th May 1962. (J. Scrace)

74. An unusual visitor on 31st January 1960 was one of the three 5-car "Brighton Belle" units, still in its traditional chocolate and cream livery. It was diverted from Victoria to London Bridge due to engineering works and is passing a stopping service to Epsom Downs. (S.C. Nash)

76. A view from the same footbridge (but through a different lens) on 29th October 1983 shows no. 73121, then recently named *Croydon 1883-1983*, hauling assorted freight wagons in connection with the preparation of new publicity material. (J.S. Petley)

77. Regrettably economic constraints have forced featureless CLASP buildings to be provided but thankfully new BR architecture has improved recently. This is the up platform in 1988 – an island platform is no longer required. (J. Scrace)

SYDENHAM

78. Opened with the line, the station was substantially rebuilt in 1853-54 during the quadrupling of the main line. Here we are looking under Sydenham Road at the up platform, sometime before the covering of sleepers with ballast was outlawed. (D. Cullum collection)

79. Photographed on 13th August 1961, these up side buildings are believed to be of L&CR origin. Alas this handsome structure was allowed to decay and has been demolished. (Pamlin Prints)

80. The up platform, from which this photograph was taken, was replaced in 1982 by a new one situated about 100 yds to the north, the crossover now being in advance of the platform. The retaining wall of the old platform was beginning to collapse and a move was the most economical option. (Pamlin Prints)

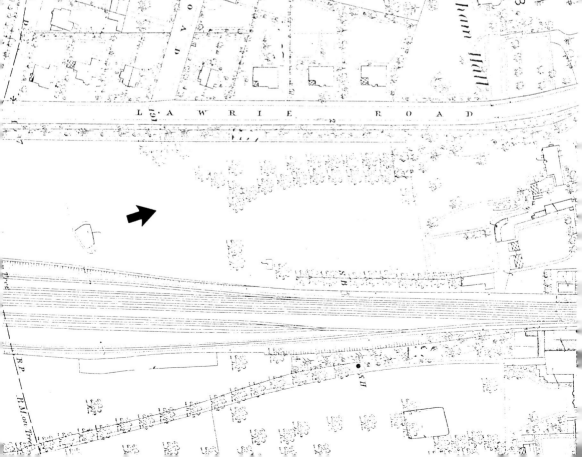

81. The exterior of the down side in 1967 bears a poster for the short-lived BR-operated hovercraft service between Portsmouth and Cowes. This is one of the few historic buildings to survive on the route. (E. Jackson collection)

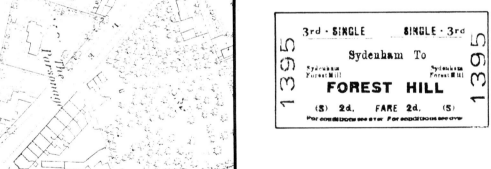

XV. The 1870 edition shows the station to be mainly serving mansions set in wooded grounds. The Crystal Palace branch diverges south of the platforms.

82. The down side was rebuilt in 1875 but the canopy is a recent replacement. This view shows the new steel footbridge and spartan up side facilities. (J. Scrace)

83. The down line to Crystal Palace is carried over the main quadruple tracks on a flyover, the girders of which appear on the left of this picture. The train is empty stock from New Cross Gate to Crystal Palace hauled by class W no. 31919 on 26th June 1954. The up connection is in the foreground. (S.C. Nash)

PENGE WEST

84. Opened with the line, the station closed in about 1841 but was reopened on 1st July 1863 as "Penge Bridges". The suffix was dropped in 1879 and "west" was added in July 1923. This is the approach from Dulwich Road, now the High Street. (Lens of Sutton)

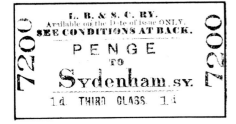

85. The yellow brick building, with its up-turned canopy, on the up platform (left) remained in use in 1988 but the structure opposite has been demolished.
(Lens of Sutton)

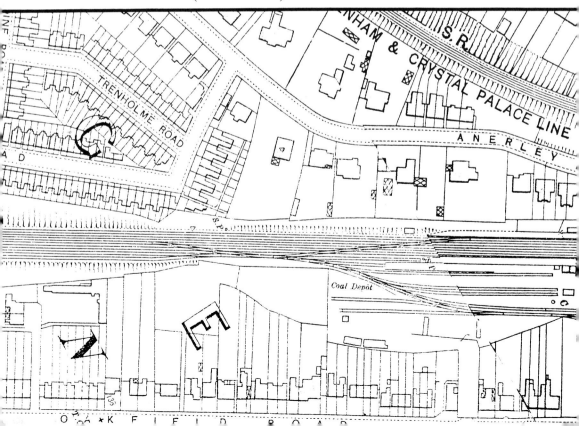

86. No. 33023 speeds south on 11th August 1982 with the 17.34 London Bridge to East Grinstead. It will have just passed over the former LCDR Bromley - Herne Hill route. East Grinstead services were electrified in October 1987. (J. Scrace)

XVI. The 1933 map shows the proximity of the Crystal Palace line and the goods yard, which closed on 4th May 1964. The signal box was shut on 21st August 1966.

ANERLEY

87. One of the original stations, it was initially spelt Annerley (Lonely Place) after the nearby home of Mr. William Sanderson. Class C2 no. 540 passes the buffers of the headshunt of Penge yard, visible at the end of the platform. (J.R.W. Kirkby collection)

88. The tracks are on embankment between Penge and Anerley where the station is in a shallow cutting. The first buildings were demolished during the quadrupling of 1853-54 and the station was rebuilt again in 1875. (P. Rutherford)

89. A northward view under Anerley Road in April 1968 shows the generous canopies no longer deemed economic. A new small office has recently been built in brick on the down side. Anerley Box was to the left of the camera until 1950. (British Rail)

90. A SAGA holiday train from Newcastle, bound for Eastbourne, passes through on 7th September 1985, the last year in which it ran. It had travelled via Clapham Junction and Crystal Palace into London Bridge, where it reversed and dropped holidaymakers bound for Folkestone. (J.S. Petley)

91. A March 1987 picture includes interesting details of the charming station house, such as the cast iron lattice windows. It is a reminder of the rural environment that existed in the early years of the railway. (A.C. Mott)

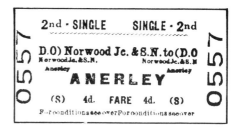

NORWOOD JUNCTION LOCOMOTIVE SHED

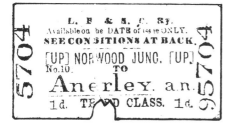

92. Opened in 1935, the depot was bounded by the down Crystal Palace - Norwood Junction line (right) and the main line, the up signals of which are seen on the left, in this August 1963 view. The flyover carrying the former over the latter is obscured by the covered coal stage. The three lines between it and the water tank lead to the turntable. (J. Scrace)

93. Up to 50 steam locomotives were allocated here, mainly for freight work. Diesels were on the increase when class E6 no. 32413 was photographed on the 65 ft. turntable in 1958. (F.W. Ivey)

94. Former LSWR no. 120 and Caledonian Railway no. 123 were being prepared for a special train from Victoria on 15th September 1963, as Stewarts Lane shed had closed the previous week. This shed ceased to function in January 1964 and the site is now used as a cable store by the CM&EE. (S.C. Nash)

NORWOOD JUNCTION

95. "Jolly Sailor" was the cheery name given to the station from the opening of the line until October 1846. In 1859, it was resited 80 yds. southwards and this up side building is believed to date from that time and remains in use today. (Lens of Sutton)

96. Class E3 no. 457 *Watersfield* was named after a village near Pulborough in Sussex and demonstrates the attention paid to engine cleanliness, even on a humble New Cross freight service. (J.R.W. Kirkby collection)

97. The 8.45 am Brighton to London Bridge, commonly called the "City Limited" was derailed on 1st May 1891, due to the failure of the bridge over Portland Road. Behind the van were four first-class six-wheelers followed by a bogie-first and the Pullman *Jupiter*. Only five injuries resulted. The lines in the foreground are from Beckenham Junction LCDR. (E.R. Lacey collection)

98. The engine involved in the accident was Gladstone B1 class no. 175 *Hayling*, then less than six months old. In the background is Goat House bridge. (E.R. Lacey collection)

99. A third photograph taken on the same day was shot from the defective bridge, looking at the north end of the station and including class E tanks no. 110 *Burgundy* and no. 146 *Havre*. (E.R. Lacey collection)

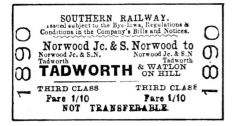

100. Although the locomotive is not clear, this photograph does show North Box better than in picture no. 97. It is also interesting to compare the signals with those in picture no. 99. A class B4 hauls a down special to Portsmouth via the Quarry line and Three Bridges. (Lens of Sutton)

XVII. The 1913 survey has the London Bridge lines on the right and the double track spur to Beckenham Junction below them. These merge to single line in the station, the entire spur being singled in 1928 and closed on 30th October 1966. Norwood Yard and Selhurst Depot are to the left.

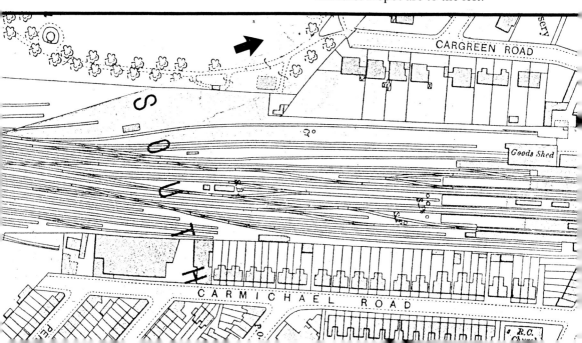

101. A photograph from 18th December 1926 shows class E5X no. B576 with a down train under the AC wires, not long before conductor rails were laid. "South Norwood" was officially added on 1st October 1910. (H.C. Casserley)

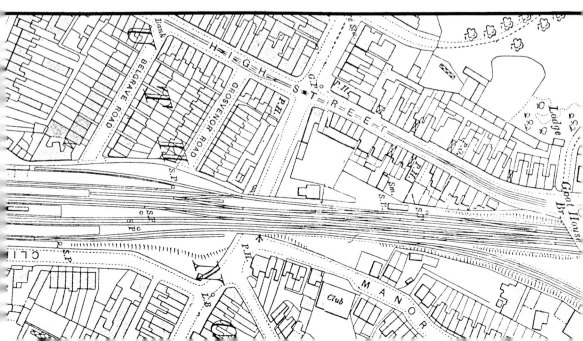

102. On the left is the goods shed, which was still standing in 1988. This post-WWII view shows platforms 1, 2 and 3 which were and are used by up trains. Note that 1 and 2 have a common track – less of a problem since the introduction of stock with sliding doors. (Lens of Sutton)

SOUTHERN RAILWAY.
Issued subject to the Bye-laws, Regulations &
Conditions in the Company's Bills and Notices.

Norwood Jc. & S. Norwood to
Norwood Junction   Norwood Junction
E. or W. Croydon   E. or W. Croydon
or Thornton Heath   or Thornton Heath
EAST or WEST CROYDON
or THORNTON HEATH
THIRD CLASS   THIRD CLASS
Fare 4d.   Fare 4d.
N   TRANSFERABLE

103. The LBSCR North Box on stilts was replaced by this lower design which remained in use until 21st March 1954. (British Rail)

104. Looking south from platform 3 on 6th March 1954, we see the new box which replaced South Box, visible beyond it. It also replaced North Box two weeks later. Colour light signals were controlled from the new box southwards to East Croydon North Box. Three Bridges panel took over this area on 8th April 1984. (D. Cullum)

105. Looking north on the same day, the new signals are ready for use but the platforms are still lit by gas. On the right is "The Signal", a public house since renamed the "Portmanor". (D. Cullum)

106. The "Gatwick Express" runs every 15 minutes to and from Victoria but normally via Selhurst. Introduced in May 1984, it is seen on 27th September 1986, having run via Crystal Palace, due to engineering work. The non-electrified line on the right leads to the disused platform 7. (A. Dasi-Sutton)

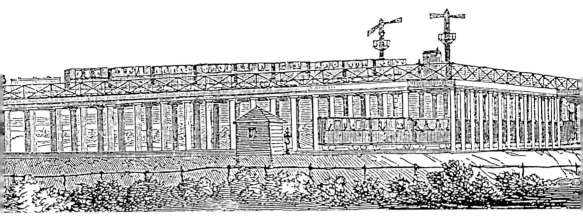

XVIII. A third track for atmospheric trains was on the east side of the main line and so a flyover (probably the first in the world) was built of timber to carry it over the L&BR lines, the tube presenting almost insuperable problems at junctions. A piston car (devoid of the valve closing and heating car) is seen descending towards Norwood, hauling ordinary coaches, while a Brighton bound train passes underneath.

107. Looking south from a point close to Norwood Fork Box in 1937, we have the line to Selhurst (right foreground); the West Croydon lines (right distance) and the main East Croydon tracks in the centre. (British Rail)

108. Another southward view shows Norwood Fork Box shortly before it was closed on 21st March 1954. Its successor, Gloucester Road Junction Box, is seen on the right. Diagrams XXI and XXIII in our *Victoria to East Croydon* album clarify this complex junction. (D. Cullum)

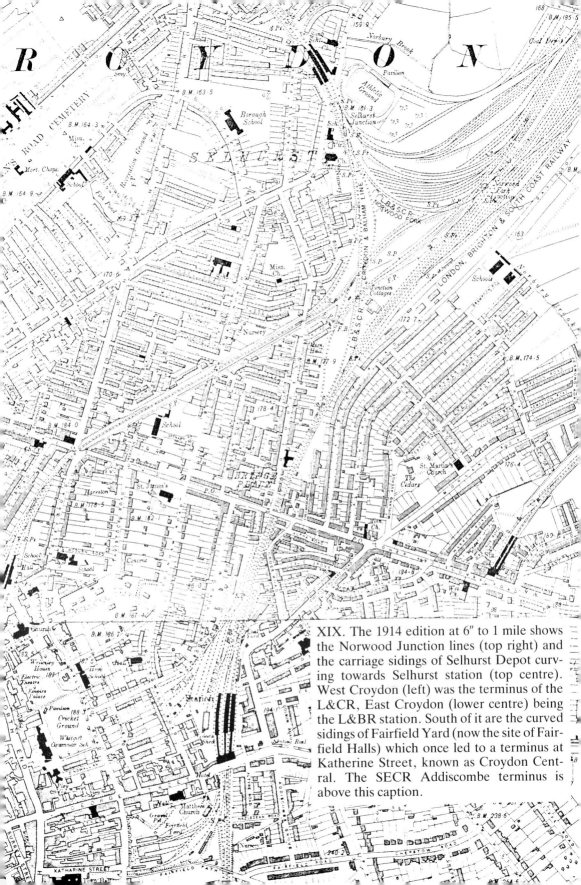

XIX. The 1914 edition at 6″ to 1 mile shows the Norwood Junction lines (top right) and the carriage sidings of Selhurst Depot curving towards Selhurst station (top centre). West Croydon (left) was the terminus of the L&CR, East Croydon (lower centre) being the L&BR station. South of it are the curved sidings of Fairfield Yard (now the site of Fairfield Halls) which once led to a terminus at Katherine Street, known as Croydon Central. The SECR Addiscombe terminus is above this caption.

109. Windmill Bridge Junction is the southern most of the group of junctions and closest to East Croydon. Class C no. A33 proceeds from Norwood Junction towards East Croydon on 13th April 1925. On the left is Gloucester Road Junction Box close to the Victoria line, with its overhead electric gantries. (W.H. Whitworth)

110. A northward view from St. James's Road bridge in July 1923 includes Windmill Bridge Junction Box and its signal bridge in the background. The tracks were (from left to right) – up, down, up, down and down relief. (Late E. Wallis)

EAST CROYDON

111. Initially just double track was provided and in 1862 an additional pair of lines were laid on the west side for local trains. These terminated in separate platforms known as "New Croydon". The local lines were extended south in 1865 and the resulting fragmented station was rebuilt in 1894 with a single frontage, still in use in 1988.
(Lens of Sutton)

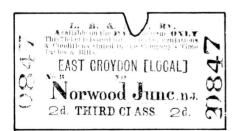

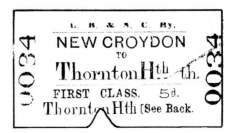

112. Class B4 no.59 waits in the up main loop while a class E1 0-6-0T runs into the middle siding. Typical LBSCR signals abound although the photograph was taken after 1st April 1925 when overhead electrification was extended from Balham to Coulsdon North. (J.R.W. Kirkby collection)

113. Taken sometime after the grouping, this photograph shows class E4 no. B520. The "Elevated Electric" behind, still in LBSCR colours, is starting back from the down local platform and the picture was therefore probably taken on a Sunday, when some Crystal Palace trains were extended to and from East Croydon.
(J.R.W. Kirkby collection)

114. "11" indicated Coulsdon North via Streatham on these five car electric sets, in which the middle vehicle was a motorised bogie van, with bow collectors. The signal by North Box is off, ready for class C no. A723 to depart, on 18th February 1926.
(H.C. Casserley)

115. Hall & Co., builders merchants, had their own siding north of the station, its gates being visible right of centre in this north-looking view from July 1935. No. 2594 was named *Shortbridge* by the LBSCR and was the class E5 used for push-pull experiments in 1938. (J.G. Sturt)

116. The 2.30 pm London Bridge to Maidstone West hop pickers' special approaches platform 6 on 9th September 1950, headed by ex-SECR E class no. 1547. Entire families of Londoners camped on Kent farms for the short picking season every year, generating much extra rail traffic. The vans carried numerous old prams loaded with camping equipment. (J.J. Smith)

117. The busy goods shed faced platform 1 and remained in use until May 1973, but was not demolished until 1986. A Scammell mechanical horse is seen alongside a real one. (E. Jackson)

118. Semaphore signalling ceased on 21st March 1954 when colour lights were brought into use south of Norwood Junction North Box. The locomotive water tank is visible, as is Windmill Bridge Junction up distant in the off position – a rare sight. (Pamlin Prints)

Other maps and photographs are to be found in our *Victoria to East Croydon* and *East Croydon to Three Bridges* albums.

119. The 11.45 special from Gatwick Airport to London Bridge leaves platform 2 with no. 73101 *Brighton Evening Argus* at the rear on 25th April 1984. The air conditioned stock was on passenger evaluation. In the distance is the 1955 signal box which became redundant on 7th April 1984, since when all movements have been controlled from Three Bridges. (J. Scrace)

120. The bridge in the background carries a mailbag conveyor which links the adjacent sorting office with each platform, making the dock on the right obsolete. Photographed in 1986, this class 455 unit was on the stopping service to Caterham. Since May 1988 two local trains each hour from Purley have been extended to Luton, being operated by similar class 319 units which have the added advantage of a toilet. (A.C. Mott)

MP Middleton Press

Easebourne Lane, Midhurst, West Sussex, GU29 9AZ
☎ Midhurst (073 081) 3169

BRANCH LINES
BRANCH LINES TO MIDHURST
BRANCH LINES TO HORSHAM
BRANCH LINES TO EAST GRINSTEAD
BRANCH LINES TO ALTON
BRANCH LINE TO HAYLING
BRANCH LINE TO SOUTHWOLD
BRANCH LINE TO TENTERDEN
BRANCH LINES TO NEWPORT
BRANCH LINES TO TUNBRIDGE WELLS
BRANCH LINE TO SWANAGE
BRANCH LINES TO LONGMOOR
BRANCH LINES TO LYME REGIS
BRANCH LINES **AROUND** MIDHURST
BRANCH LINE TO FAIRFORD

SOUTH COAST RAILWAYS
BRIGHTON TO WORTHING
WORTHING TO CHICHESTER
CHICHESTER TO PORTSMOUTH
BRIGHTON TO EASTBOURNE
RYDE TO VENTNOR
EASTBOURNE TO HASTINGS
PORTSMOUTH TO SOUTHAMPTON
HASTINGS TO ASHFORD*
SOUTHAMPTON TO BOURNEMOUTH
ASHFORD TO DOVER

COUNTRY RAILWAY ROUTES
BOURNEMOUTH TO EVERCREECH JUNCTION
READING TO GUILDFORD

SOUTHERN MAIN LINES
WOKING TO PORTSMOUTH
HAYWARDS HEATH TO SEAFORD
EPSOM TO HORSHAM
CRAWLEY TO LITTLEHAMPTON
THREE BRIDGES TO BRIGHTON
WATERLOO TO WOKING
VICTORIA TO EAST CROYDON
TONBRIDGE TO HASTINGS
EAST CROYDON TO THREE BRIDGES
WOKING TO SOUTHAMPTON
WATERLOO TO WINDSOR
LONDON BRIDGE TO EAST CROYDON

STEAMING THROUGH
STEAMING THROUGH KENT
STEAMING THROUGH EAST HANTS
STEAMING THROUGH EAST SUSSEX
STEAMING THROUGH SURREY
STEAMING THROUGH WEST SUSSEX
STEAMING THROUGH THE
   ISLE OF WIGHT

OTHER RAILWAY BOOKS
WAR ON THE LINE
(Reprint of the SR history in World War II)
GARRAWAY FATHER AND SON
(Biography - includes LNER, Talyllyn and Festiniog Railways)

OTHER BOOKS
MIDHURST TOWN – THEN & NOW
EAST GRINSTEAD – THEN & NOW
THE MILITARY DEFENCE OF WEST SUSSEX
WEST SUSSEX WATERWAYS
SURREY WATERWAYS
BATTLE OVER PORTSMOUTH
A City at war in 1940
SUSSEX POLICE FORCES

*Video also available. Details from
M.P. Videos, 11 Park Crescent, Midhurst,
West Sussex GU29 9ED.